Alexis Smith
An Embarrassment of Riches

March 21 - April 21, 2001

Lawrence Rubin • Greenberg Van Doren • Fine Art

730 Fifth Avenue, at 57th Street
New York NY 10019
212 - 445 - 0444 TELEPHONE
212 - 445 - 0442 FAX

PLATE 1

LA-Z-BOY

2001

mixed media collage

20 7/8 x 24 7/8 x 2 inches

The simple life.

An Embarrassment of Riches: A Brief Conversation between Alexis Smith and Amy Gerstler

AG: When I look at this new work, I can't help thinking that this show is a rather non-judgmental critique of current materialistic American culture.

AS: Well, this body of work deals with the idea that most humans spend a lot of time thinking about things that they lack, and feel that if they possessed, then they'd finally be happy. It seems like part of the human condition to be perpetually prey to that kind of yearning. Some of the things we long for in this way are actual tangible objects, and some are intangibles. *If only I had —— you fill in the blank: a husband, a mink coat, a million dollars, a promotion, a facelift, a chocolate sundae, then I'd be ok, feel better, be at peace.*

I think Americans especially tend to think in terms of material things having the power to make them happy. Right now in American culture, advertising, making money, and the notion that buying things is a way of gaining not only status but happiness and worthiness seems very dominant. In terms of material objects serving as expressions of people's aspirations, the home seems like a really big focus these days: all the emphasis on real estate, furnishings, cooking and gardening as exemplified in magazines like *House & Garden* and *Gourmet*. Making your home an example, a showcase of your good taste, or wearing the right designer clothes, or driving the right car – the implication seems to be that if you know what the things of quality are, then that knowledge is supposed to confer on *you* as a person a certain level of quality, a sort of cachet...

I'm particularly interested in what relations these ideas about quality and good taste set up between us and material objects. My own experience is that people are often oppressed by their desires, by the things that they covet. Two of the quotes in the show, the one from Emerson, "Things are in the saddle and ride mankind," and the proverb, "Everyone is a master and servant," seem to make that point, that you can try to control some things in life, but there are other things that control you. An example from my own life is that there was a period when I badly wanted to have a husband and a house – I was longing for a more domestic way of life. When I was married and got that wish, and saw how much trouble was attached to owning property and so on, I almost wished that Scott and I could go back to a simpler way of living, that we could move back into the studio with the loft and the hotplate and regain that more carefree, scruffy way of living that had begun to seem like the halcyon days.

It's an ageless question: *How come people are never satisfied, no matter what?* When you realize that the things you want usually only make you feel satisfied for a short period of time, it's really a hard life lesson. Physical experiences — no matter how "peak" — don't seem to have much content except what you project on them. The idea of what is valuable, what is crucial, what things are worth and what gives them that worth is central to what I was thinking about in making this work.

It's funny because these issues relate directly to my method of working. I pick stuff up out of the street, maybe even out of the trash, things of ostensibly no value and then I imbue them with value by making them into art, by pairing them with text and putting them into a context that changes their value completely. These are the peculiarly magical transformations that supposedly worthless objects undergo when they become part of my artwork. Because I work this way, picking up devalued and/or discarded objects and re-infusing them with value by changing their role in the world, I'm probably even more dubious about the idea that material acquisitions can equal happiness, because it all seems so relative and chancy.

AG: This skepticism frequently comes across as wry humor.

AS: I agree that there is humor in this show and in all my work, but it's partly a byproduct of the medium. Collage particularly lends itself to the unexpected contrasts and juxtapositions which make it possible to generate this kind of humor and an attendant ambiguity that is important to me. The viewer is always put in an ambiguous position because there are polar extremes contained within each piece, and not necessarily reconciled at all. Viewers have to decide which pole to gravitate towards, because the artist isn't telling them how to resolve these contradictions. There's a kind of lack of judgement implied, and that's the point. Nobody is being "wrong" or "bad" in the view the artwork presents. This is just how human beings are. The artwork has the ability to contain these contrasts or extremes without having to side with one or the other.

AG: Alex, what you're talking about sounds like Keats' famous definition of "negative capability," which I think he defined as "capable of being in uncertainties, mysteries, doubts, without any irritable reaching after fact and reason."

AS: I hope that's true. I am definitely sure that none of us are immune to embarrassing human foibles, and there are certain timeless and constant aspects of human experience that are almost unavoidably difficult and hard to resolve. It's those ahistorical or archetypal yearnings and desires and their accompanying disappointments and frustrations that I find so endlessly fascinating, and that I like to ponder through the vehicle of my work. I think my work comes directly out of this collision between the things I'm thinking about and the physical objects in my studio, and it always surprises and frightens me a little because I don't know what it means until after the fact.

AG: There is another relevant quote that you always hear in poetry classes, "No ideas but in things." [1]

AS: Yes, that's it exactly.

Amy Gerstler is a writer and long time collaborator with the artist. Their joint projects include *Past Lives*, an installation and artist's book, 1989, and *The Sorcerer's Apprentice*, installation, 2000.

[1]. William Carlos Williams

PLATE 2

House & Garden

2001

mixed media collage

26 3/4 x 23 x 3 1/4 inches

Every bird thinks its own nest charming.

PLATE 3

The Best of All Possible Worlds
2001
mixed media collage
27 1/4 x 27 1/4 x 3 1/2 inches

Tout est pour le mieux dans le meilleur des mondes possibles.

PLATE 4

Town & Country
2001
mixed media collage on folding table
36 3/4 x 28 x 5 1/2 inches

Things are in the saddle and ride mankind.

PLATE 5
Hunter's Guide
2001
mixed media collage
23 1/4 x 19 3/4 x 1 1/2 inches

HUNTER (Old English). One who hunts for food and entertainment.

PLATE 6

Cachet

2001

mixed media collage

24 3/8 x 21 1/8 x 1 1/2 inches

We want to buy the right stuff, but we don't necessarily know what it is.

PLATE 7

Emancipation

2001

mixed media collage

25 x 20 x 2 ¾ inches

Everyone is a master and servant.

PLATE 8

Pursuit of Happiness

2001

mixed media collage

26 3/8 x 34 1/4 x 3 1/8 inches

PLATE 9

Forbidden Fruit

2001

mixed media collage

29 3/8 x 25 1/4 x 1 3/4 inches

What sells is hope.

PLATE 10
An Embarrassment of Riches
2001
mixed media collage
23 1/8 x 27 1/8 x 4 1/4 inches

PLATE 11

Fantasyland

2001

mixed media

45 x 39 x 2 3/8 inches

A dream is a wish your heart makes.

PLATE 12

Vanity Fair
2001
mixed media collage
32 x 41 x 1 3/4 inches

Every woman would rather be beautiful than good.

PLATE 13

Love Never Faileth

2001

mixed media collage

22 x 18 3/8 x 2 1/4 inches

PLATE 14
Wild Thing
2001
mixed media collage
22 1/2 x 18 1/2 x 1 1/2 inches

Wild Thing

PLATE 15

No Exit

2001

mixed media collage

44 3/4 × 36 3/4 × 2 1/4 inches

Everybody have red blood and salty tear.

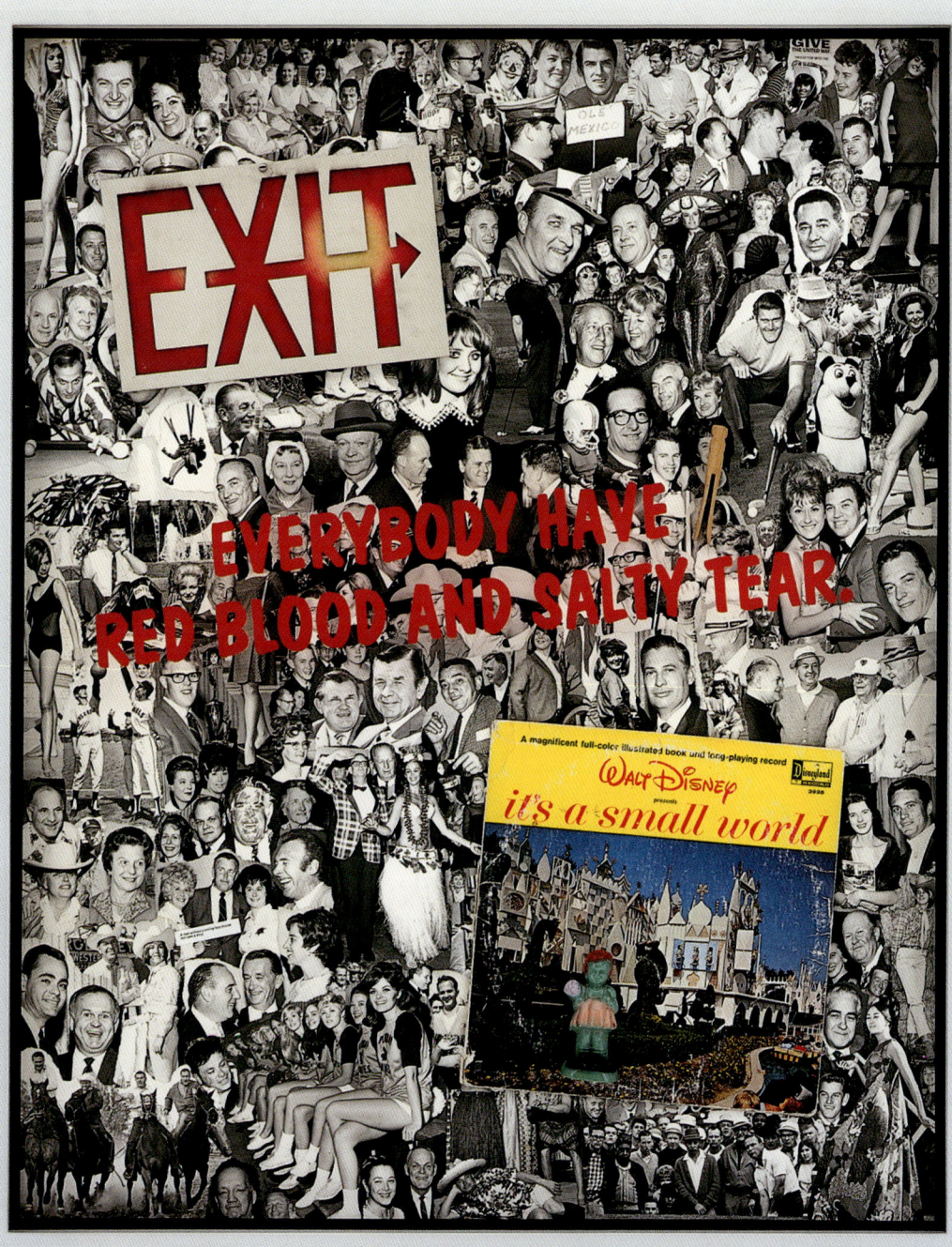

ALEXIS SMITH

BORN

1949
Los Angeles, California
Lives and works in Los Angeles, California

EDUCATION

1970
University of California at Irvine, CA, B.A.

SELECTED SOLO EXHIBITIONS

2001
An Embarrassment of Riches, Lawrence Rubin · Greenberg Van Doren · Fine Art, NY
The Sorcerer's Apprentice, with Amy Gerstler, Museum of Contemporary Art, San Diego, CA

2000
The Sorcerer's Apprentice, with Amy Gerstler, Miami Art Museum, Miami, FL
Fools Rush In, Ameringer Howard, Boca Raton, FL

1999
Words to Live By, Margo Leavin Gallery, Los Angeles, CA

1997
My Favorite Sport, Wexner Art Center, Ohio State University, Columbus, OH
A Matter of Taste, J. Paul Getty Museum, Los Angeles, CA

1995
Alexis Smith: The Farmer's Daughter, Gerald Peters Gallery, Dallas, TX
Alexis Smith: Cherished Notions, Margo Leavin Gallery, Los Angeles, CA

1994
Alexis Smith: The Wonder Years, 1973-1983, Margo Leavin Gallery, Los Angeles, CA

1993
Alexis Smith, Margo Leavin Gallery, Los Angeles, CA
Looking for America, Pasadena City College Art Gallery, Pasadena, CA

1991
Alexis Smith: Public Works, Mandeville Gallery, University of California, San Diego, CA
Alexis Smith, Whitney Museum of American Art, New York, NY; traveled to: The Museum of Contemporary Art, Los Angeles, CA

1990
Eldorado (On the Road, Part II), Margo Leavin Gallery, Los Angeles, CA

1989
Past Lives, with Amy Gerstler, Santa Monica Museum of Art, CA; traveled to: Josh Baer Gallery, New York, NY

1988
On The Road, Margo Leavin Gallery, Los Angeles, CA

1987
Same Old Paradise, Grand Lobby installation, The Brooklyn Museum, Brooklyn, NY
Art and the Law, Bar Association of San Francisco, San Francisco, CA; traveled to: Albrecht Art Museum, St. Joseph, MO; Muscarelle Museum of Art, College of William & Mary, Williamsburg, VA; Minnesota Museum of Art, St. Paul, MN
Alexis Smith - Joseph Cornell: Parallels, Aspen Art Museum, Aspen, CO

1986
Viewpoints: Alexis Smith, Walker Art Center, Minneapolis, MN
Currents: Alexis Smith, The Institute of Contemporary Art, Boston, MA

1985
Alexis Smith: Jane, Margo Leavin Gallery, Los Angeles, CA

1982
Christmas Eve, 1943, Margo Leavin Gallery, Los Angeles, CA
Chinese Junk, Clocktower, New York, NY
Satan's Satellites, Rosamund Felsen Gallery, Los Angeles, CA

1981
U.S.A., Holly Solomon Gallery, New York, NY
Stardust, Bing Theater, Los Angeles County Museum of Art, Los Angeles, CA
Stardust, La Jolla Museum of Contemporary Art, CA

1980
Raymond Chandler's L.A., Rosamund Felsen Gallery, Los Angeles, CA
Stardust, performance with Heide Hardin, Los Angeles Contemporary Exhibitions, Los Angeles, CA

1979
The Room on the Other Side of the Mirror, installation, Foundation de Appel, Amsterdam
The Magic Mountain, Holly Solomon Gallery, New York, NY
Autumn Sonata, window installation, LAICA Downtown Window, Los Angeles, CA

1978
April Foole, Holly Solomon Gallery, New York, NY
The Art of Magic, Close-up, performance with Tony DeLap, Baxter Art Gallery, California Institute of Technology, Pasadena, CA
The Magic Mountain and *Medium*, performance, Rosamund Felsen Gallery, Los Angeles, CA

1977
Tales of Mystery and Enchantment, Nicholas Wilder Gallery, Los Angeles, CA
Alexis Smith, Holly Solomon Gallery, New York, NY

1976
Alexis Smith, San Jose State University, San Jose, CA
Star Material, Mandeville Art Gallery, University of California at San Diego, San Diego, CA
Scherherezade the Storyteller, performance, CARP, Los Angeles, CA

1975
Anteroom, installation, CARP, Los Angeles, CA
Rapido, installation, Art Galleries, University of California at Santa Barbara, Santa Barbara, CA
Alexis Smith, Whitney Museum of American Art, New York, NY
Classics Illustrated, Long Beach Museum of Art, Long Beach, CA

1974
Alexis Smith, Riko Mizuno Gallery, Los Angeles, CA

SELECTED GROUP EXHIBITIONS

2001 *Beau Monde: Toward a Redeemed Conceptualism*, SITE Santa Fe International Biennial, Santa Fe, NM
Evidence of Love; Romance, Desire & Fantasy, Jack Rutberg Fine Arts, Inc., Los Angeles, CA
Postmodern Americans: A Selection, The Menil Collection, Houston, TX
A Way with Words: Selections from the Whitney Museum of American Art, Whitney Museum of American Art at Philip Morris, New York, NY

2000 *Made in California*, Los Angeles County Museum of Art, Los Angeles, CA
Library, Margo Leavin Gallery, Los Angeles, CA
12 Divas, Molly Barnes Gallery, Los Angeles, CA
The Big Go Stands for Goodness: Corita Kent's 1960s POP, Harriet and Charles Luckman Fine Arts Gallery, California State University, Los Angeles, CA; traveled to: Nora Eccles Harrison Museum of Art, Utah State University, Logan, UT; Donna Beam Fine Art Gallery, University of Nevada, Las Vegas, NV; Art Gallery, University of Texas, San Antonio, TX

1999 *Radical P.A.S.T.: Contemporary Art in Pasadena 1960-1974*, Armory Center for the Arts, Williamson Gallery at Art Center College of Design, and Norton Simon Museum of Art, Pasadena

1998 *90069*, Margo Leavin Gallery, Los Angeles, CA

1997 *A Singular Vision: Prints from Landfall Press*, The Museum of Modern Art, New York, NY
Sunshine & Noir: Art in L.A. 1960 - 1997, Louisiana Museum of Modern Art, Humlebaek, Denmark; traveled: to Kunstmuseum Wolfsburg, Wolfsburg, Germany; Castello di Rivoli, Turin, Italy; UCLA at the Armand Hammer Museum of Art and Cultural Center, Los Angeles, CA
Scene of the Crime, UCLA at the Armand Hammer Museum of Art and Cultural Center, Los Angeles, CA

1996 *Continuity & Contradiction*, Museum of Contemporary Art, San Diego, La Jolla, CA
Blurring the Boundaries: Installation Art 1970-1996, Museum of Contemporary Art, San Diego, CA, and Memorial Art Gallery, Rochester, NY; traveled to: Worcester Art Museum, MA; Ringling Museum of Art, Sarasota, FL; Scottsdale Center for the Arts, AZ; Davenport Art Museum, IA; University of Texas, Austin, TX; San Jose Museum of Art, CA; Marco Museo de Arte Contemporaneo, Monterry, Mexico; Delaware Art Museum, Wilmington, DE

1995 *Untitled (Reading Room)*, Margo Leavin Gallery, Los Angeles, CA
25 Years: An Exhibition of Selected Works, Margo Leavin Gallery, Los Angeles, CA
Art Works: The PaineWebber Collection of Contemporary Masters, Museum of Fine Arts, Houston, TX; traveled to: Detroit Institute of Arts, MI; Museum of Fine Arts, Boston, MA; Minneapolis Institute of Arts, MN; San Diego Museum of Art, CA; Center for the Fine Arts, Miami, FL

1994 *Elvis + Marilyn: 2 x Immortal*, Institute of Contemporary Art, Boston, MA; traveled to: Contemporary Art Museum, Houston, TX; Mint Museum of Art, Charlotte, NC; Cleveland Museum of Art, OH; Jacksonville Museum of Contemporary Art, FL; Portland Art Museum, OR; Philbrook Museum of Art, Tulsa, OK; Columbus Museum of Art, OH; Tennessee State Museum, Nashville, TN; San Jose Museum of Art, CA, Honolulu Academy of Art, HI
Romance, Alyce de Roulet Williamson Gallery, Art Center College of Design, Pasadena, CA

1993 *Picasso to Christo: The Evolution of a Collection*, Santa Barbara Museum of Art, CA
A Complete Hand of One Suit, Donna Beam Fine Art Gallery, University of Nevada, Las Vegas
Western Myth: Twentieth Century Update, Aspen Art Museum, CO
Collage and Assemblage, Lennon, Weinberg, Inc., New York, NY

1992 *Proof: Los Angeles Art and the Photograph, 1960-1980*, Laguna Art Museum, Laguna Beach, CA
Connections: Explorations in the Getty Center Collections, The Getty Center for the History of Art and the Humanities, Santa Monica, CA
The Edge of Childhood, The Heckscher Museum, New York, NY
Hollywood, Hollywood, Alyce de Roulet Williamson Gallery, Art Center College of Design, Pasadena, CA

1991 *A Passion for Art / Watercolors and Works on paper*, Tony Shafrazi Gallery, New York, NY
Addiction, Santa Barbara Contemporary Arts Forum, CA
Transforming the Western Image in 20th Century American Art, Palm Springs Desert Museum, Palm Springs, CA; traveled to: Boise Art Museum, ID; Tucson Museum of Art, AZ; The Rockwell Museum, Corning, NY
Songs of Innocence Songs of Experience, Whitney Museum of American Art at Equitable Center, New York, NY
20th Century Collage, Margo Leavin Gallery, Los Angeles, CA; traveled to: Centro Cultural Arte Contemporaneo, Mexico City, Mexico; Musee d'Art Moderne et d'Art Contemporain, Nice, France
Framed, Stephen Wirtz Gallery, San Francisco, CA

1990 *Word as Image: American Art 1960-1990*, Miwaukee Art Museum, WI; traveled to: Oklahoma City Art; Museum, OK; Contemporary Arts Museum, Houston, TX
Crossing the Line: Word and Image in Art, 1960-1990, Montgomery Gallery, Pomona College, Claremont, CA

1989 *Image World: Art and Media Culture*, Whitney Museum of American Art, New York, NY
Selections from the Beatrice and Philip Gersh Collection, The Museum of Contemporary Art, Los Angeles, CA
Constructing a History: A Focus on MOCA's Permanent Collection, The Museum of Contemporary Art, Los Angeles, CA
Making Their Mark: Women Artists Move into the Mainstream, 1970-85, Cincinnati Art Museum, OH; traveled to: New Orleans Museum of Art, LA; Denver Art Museum, Denver, CO, Pennsylvania Academy of the Fine Arts, PA
Forty Years of California Assemblage, Wight Art Gallery, University of California, Los Angeles, CA; traveled to: San Jose Museum of Art, CA; Fresno Art Museum, CA; Joslyn Art Museum, Omaha, NE
A Brave New World: John Baldessari/Vernon Fisher/ Stephen Prina/Ed Ruscha/ Alexis Smith, Karsten Schubert Ltd., London

1988 *Striking Distance*, The Museum of Contemporary Art, Los Angeles, CA; traveled to: Triton Museum of Art, Santa Clara, CA; Fresno Art Museum, CA Auto-Perceptions: Los Angeles Artists and the Car, Gallery 1220, Perloff Hall, University of California, Los Angeles, CA
Layers: Media and Culture, Hewlett Gallery, Carnegie Mellon University, Pittsburgh, PA

1987 *Contemporary American Collage, 1960-1985*, Herter Art Gallery, University of Massachusetts, Amherst, MA; traveled to: Benson Museum of Art, University of Connecticut, Storrs, CT; Lehigh University Gallery, Bethlahem, PA; American Art, Youngstown, OH; Stedman Art Gallery, Rutgers University Camden, NJ; Johnson Museum of Art, Cornell University, Ithaca, NY; University of Nevada, Las Vegas, NV
Avant-Garde in the Eighties, installation, Los Angeles County Museum of Art, Los Angeles, CA
Concept/reality: Los Angeles Public Art, University Art Gallery, Pepperdine University, Malibu, CA
Comic iconoclasm, Institute of Contemporary Arts, London
Selections from the Frederick R. Weisman Collection, Museum of the Pennsylvania Academy of the Fine Arts, Philadelphia, PA

1986 *Individuals: A Selected History of Contemporary Art 1945-1986*, The Museum of Contemporary Art, Los Angeles, CA
Passages: A Survey of California Women Artists, 1945 to Present, Fresno Arts Center and Museum, CA
Remembrances of Things Past, Long Beach Museum of Art, CA
Text & Image: The Wording of American Art, Holly Solomon Gallery, New York, NY
Spectrum: In other words, The Corcoran Gallery of Art, Washington DC
Contemporary Art from Southern California, U.S. Embassy, Helsinki, Finland
Gentleman's Choice, The Woman's Building Gallery, Los Angeles, CA

1985 *Selections from the William J. Hokin Collection*, Museum of Contemporary Art, Chicago, IL
Critical Messages: The Use of Public Media for Political Art by Women, Artemisia Gallery, Chicago, IL
Selections from the Permanent Collection, Newport Harbor Art Museum, Newport Beach, CA.

1984 *Verbally Charged Images*, Queens Museum, Flushing, New York, NY; traveled to: USF Art Galleries, University of South Florida, Tampa, FL; University Art Gallery, San Diego State University, CA; Art Gallery, California State College, San Bernardino, CA; Blanden Memorial Art Museum, Fort Dodge, IA; Foster Gallery, University of Wisconsin, Eau Claire, WI
An International Survey of Recent Painting and Sculpture, The Museum of Modern Art, New York, NY
Selections from the Merry and Bill Norris Collection, Fine Arts Gallery, University of California at Irvine, CA
MacArthur Park Public Art Program: Phase I-IV, Otis Art Institute at Parsons School of Design, Los Angeles, CA

1983 *A Contemporary Collection on Loan from the Rothschild Bank, Ag, Zurich*, La Jolla Museum of Contemporary Art, CA
Contemporary Collage - Extensions, Montgomery Art Gallery, Pomona College, Pomona, CA
New Directions, 1983, Hirshhorn Museum and Sculpture Garden, Washington, DC
Exchange Between Artists: Poland - U.S.A., The Douglas Hyde Gallery, University of Dublin, Ireland
Young Talent Awards, 1963-1983, Los Angeles County Museum of Art, Los Angeles, CA
Cultural Excavations: Recent and Distant, Japanese American Cultural Center, Los Angeles, CA
Inaugural Exhibition, Holly Solomon Gallery, New York, NY
The Comic Art Show, Whitney Museum of American Art, Downtown Branch, New York, NY

1982 *Contemporary Los Angeles Artists*, Nagoya City Museum, Nagoya, Japan, Municipal Art Gallery, Los Angeles, CA

New Work, Rosamund Felsen Gallery, Los Angeles, CA
Une Experience Museographique: Echange Entre Artistes, 1931-1982, Cologne - U.S.A., Musee d'Art Moderne, Paris
The Americans: The Collage, Contemporary Arts Museum, Houston, TX
Poetic Objects, Washington Project for the Arts, Washington, DC.
Poetic Visions, Otis Art Institute at Parsons School of Design, Los Angeles, CA
Words as Images, The Renaissance Society at Bergman Gallery, The University of Chicago
Whitney Biennial, Whitney Museum of American Art, New York, NY
Humor in Art, Los Angeles Institute of Contemporary Art, Los Angeles, CA
Museum as Site: Sixteen Installations, (Cathay Installation), Los Angeles County Museum of Art, Los Angeles, CA

1980 *Views Over America*, Junior Council, The Museum of Modern Art, New York, NY
Tableau, Los Angeles Institute of Contemporary Art, Los Angeles, CA
Xmas in July, Rosamund Felsen Gallery, Los Angeles, CA
Drawings, Leo Castelli Gallery, New York, NY

1979 *Storytelling in Art*, American Foundation for the Arts Museum, Miami, FL
Whitney Biennial, Whitney Museum of American Art, New York, NY
Paper on Paper, San Francisco Museum of Art, San Francisco, CA
Decade in Review, Whitney Museum of American Art, New York, NY
Kunstler Schaufenster, Neue Galerie am Landesmuseum Joanneum, Graz, Austria

1978 *American Narrative/Story of Art, 1968-78*, Contemporary Arts Museum, Houston, TX; traveled to: Contemporary Art Center, New Orleans, LA; Winnipeg Art Gallery, Manitoba, Canada; University Art Museum, Berkeley, CA.
Paris Biennale, Musee de Nice, France and Strausbourg, France
Southern California Styles of the 60's and 70's, La Jolla Museum of Contemporary Art, CA
Narration, Institute of Contemporary Art, Boston, MA

1977 *Narrative Themes/Audio Works*, Los Angeles Institute of Contemporary Art, Los Angeles, CA
Contemporary Miniatures, Fine Arts Gallery, California State University, Los Angeles, CA
Paris Biennale, Musee d'Art Moderne, Paris
The American Section of the Paris Biennale, Hudson River Museum, Yonkers, NY
Gold & Silver, Holly Solomon Gallery, New York, NY

1976 *Via Los Angeles: Asher, Burden, C. Davis, Hunt, Ruppersberg, Smith*, Portland Center for the Visual Arts, OR
AutobiographiCalifornial Fantasies, Los Angeles Institute of Contemporary Art, Los Angeles, CA
Southland Video Anthology, Part I, Long Beach Museum of Art, Long Beach, CA
Los Angeles, Penthouse Gallery, The Museum of Modern Art, New York, NY
New Talent/New Selections, Los Angeles County Museum of Art, Los Angeles, CA

1975 *Whitney Biennial*, Whitney Museum of American Art, New York, NY
Both Kinds: Contemporary Art From Los Angeles, University Art Museum, Berkeley, CA
Four Los Angeles Artists: Foulkes, Goode, Smith, Wheeler, Visual Arts Museum, New York, NY; traveled to: Corcoran Gallery of American Art, Washington, DC, Wadsworth Atheneum, Hartford, CT
Work, Image, Number, Sarah Lawrence College Gallery, Bronxville, NY
Visual/Verbal, The Art Galleries, University of California, Santa Barbara, CA
University of California at Irvine, 1965-75, La Jolla Museum of Contemporary Art, CA

1974 *Word Works*, Art Gallery, Mt. San Antonio College, Walnut, CA
Works Selected by Nicholas Wilder, Art Gallery, University of Nevada, Las Vegas, NV

1972 *Greater Magic, Mungar, Smith, Titus*, Art Gallery, University of California at Irvine, Irvine, CA
Margaret Lowe, Barbara Munger, Alexis Smith, Margaret Wilson, Los Angeles County Museum of Art, Los Angeles, CA
Southern California Attitudes, Pasadena Museum of Modern Art, Pasadena, CA

SELECTED EXHIBITION CATALOGUES

1997
Blurring the Boundaries: Installation Art 1970-1996, Museum of Contemporary Art, San Diego, CA.
Sunshine & Noir: Art in L.A. 1960-1997, Louisiana Museum of Modern Art, Humlebk, Denmark.

1995
25 Years, Margo Leavin Gallery, Los Angeles, CA.

1992
Hollywood, Hollywood, Alyce de Roulet Williamson Gallery, Art Center College of Design, Pasadena, CA.
Proof: Los Angeles Art and the Photograph, 1960-1990, Laguna Art Museum, Laguna Beach, CA.

1991
Alexis Smith: Public Works, University of California, San Diego, Mandeville Gallery, La Jolla, CA.
Alexis Smith Retrospective, Whitney Museum of American Art, New York, NY.
Transforming the Western Image in Twentieth Century American Art, Palm Springs Desert Museum, Palm Springs, CA.

1990
Crossing the Line: Word and Image in Art 1960-1990, Montgomery Gallery, Pomona College, Claremont, CA.

1989
Making Their Mark: Women Artists Move into the Mainstream, 1970-85, Cincinnati Art Museum, OH.
Forty Years of California Assemblage, Wight Art Gallery, University of California, Los Angeles.
Art in the Public Eye: Selected Developments, Security Pacific Gallery, Costa Mesa, CA.
A Brave New World: John Baldessari/Vernon Fisher//Stephen Prina/Ed Ruscha/Alexis Smith, Karsten Schubert Ltd., London.
Image World: Art and Media Culture, Whitney Museum of American Art, New York, NY.
Selections from the Beatrice and Philip Gersh Collection, The Museum of Contemporary Art, Los Angeles.

1987
Avant-Garde in the Eighties, Los Angeles County Museum of Art, Los Angeles.

1986
Viewpoint: Alexis Smith, Walker Art Center, Minneapolis.
Rememberances of Things Past, Long Beach Museum of Art, CA.
Individuals: A Selected History in Contemporary Art 1945-1986, Installation, The Museum of Contemporary Art, Los Angeles.

1985
Jane, Margo Leavin Gallery, Los Angeles.
Selections from the William J. Hokin Collection, Museum of Contemporary Art, Chicago.

1984
Verbally Charged Images, Queens Museum, Flushing, NY.
Crime and Punishment: Reflections of Violence in Contemporary Art, Triton Museum of Art, Santa Clara, CA.
An International Survey of Recent Painting and Sculpture, The Museum of Modern Art, New York.
Selections from the Merry and Bill Norris Collection, Fine Arts Gallery, University of California, Irvine.
Macarthur Park Public Art Program: Phase I-IV, Otis Art Institute at Parsons School of Design, Los Angeles.

1983
A Contemporary Collection on Loan from the Rothschild Bank, Ag, Zurich, La Jolla Museum of Contemporary Art, CA.
Contemporary Collage — Extensions, Montgomery Art Gallery, Pomona College, Pomona, CA.
New Directions, 1983, Hirshhorn Museum and Sculpture Garden, Washington, DC.
Young Talent Awards, 1963-1983, Los Angeles County Museum of Art, Los Angeles.
Cultural Excavations: Recent and Distant, Japanese American Cultural Center, Los Angeles.
Inaugural Exhibition, Holly Solomon Gallery, New York.

1982
Une Experience Museographique: Echange Entre Artistes, 1931-1982, Cologne-U.S.A., Musee d'Art Moderne, Paris.

1981
Words as Images, The Renaissance Society at Bergman Gallery, The University of Chicago.
Whitney Biennial, Whitney Museum of American Art, New York.
Messages, Freedman Gallery, Albright College, Reading, PA.
Museum as Site: Sixteen Installations, Cathay Installation, Los Angeles County Museum of Art, Los Angeles.

1980
Tableau, Los Angeles Institute of Contemporary Art, Los Angeles.

1979
Kunstler Schaufenster, Neue Galerie am Landesmuseum Joanneum, Graz, Austria.
Words and Images, Philadelphia College of Art, Philadelphia, PA.

1978
Paris Bienniale, Strasbourg, France.
Narration, Institute of Contemporary Art, Boston.

1977
Contemporary Miniatures, Fine Arts Gallery, California State University, Los Angeles.
Paris Bienniale, Musee d'Art Moderne, Paris.
American Narrative/Story of Art, 1968-78, Contemporary Arts Museum, Houston, TX.

1976
Southland Video Anthology, Part I, Long Beach Museum of Art, CA.
New Talent/New Selections, Los Angeles County Museum of Art, Los Angeles, CA.

1975
Whitney Biennial, Whitney Museum of American Art, New York.
Both Kinds: Contemporary Art from Los Angeles, University Art Museum, Berkeley, CA.
Work, Image, Number, Sarah Lawrence College Gallery, Bronxville, NY.

1974
Word Works, Art Gallery, Mount San Antonio College, Walnut, CA.

1972
Southern California Attitudes, Pasadena Museum of Modern Art, CA.

COMMISSIONS

1999
Untitled, terrazzo floor design, Schottenstein Center Sports Arena, The Ohio State University, Columbus, OH

1997
Taste, permanent mixed media wall installation for The Restaurant at The Getty Center, Los Angeles, C1993
Untitled, terrazzo floor designs for South and West Lobbies, Los Angeles Convention Center, Los Angeles, CA, Expansion Project

1992
Untitled, mixed media permanent installation for the Alaska Building in downtown Seattle, Seattle Arts Commission, WA
Snake Path, slate and concrete installation, The Stuart Collection, University of California, San Diego, La Jolla, CA
Untitled, plaza design for downtown, Playhouse Square, Cleveland, OH

1989
Collaborative proposals for Miami International Airport, with R.M.Fischer: Concourses B and D

1986
Mini-Monuments, MacArthur Park Public Arts Program, Los Angeles, CA

1985
Niagara, granite monument, Artpark, Lewiston, NY
Proposal for mixed-media collage on painted wall, The Brooklyn Public Library's Central Library, New York

1984
California, collage works in permanent painted installation, California State Office Building, Santa Rosa, CA

1983
The Grand, 8,000 square feet permanent painted installation on three levels with collage works, Keeler Grand Foyer, De Vos Hall, Grand Center, Grand Rapids, MI

1982
There's No Place Like Home, collage works in permanent painted installation, home of Aviva and Carl Covitz, Los Angeles ,CA

1981
Starlight, collage works in permanent painted installation, Unity Savings and Loan, West Hollywood, CA

SELECTED PUBLIC COLLECTIONS

Bank of America, Los Angeles, CA
Capital Group Companies, Inc., Los Angeles, CA
The Chase Manhattan Bank, North America
The Contemporary Museum, Honolulu, HI
The Getty, Los Angeles, CA
The High Museum of Art, Atlanta, GA
Los Angeles County Museum of Art, Los Angeles, CA
The Museum of Contemporary Art, Los Angeles, CA
Museum of Contemporary Art, San Diego, CA
The Museum of Modern Art, New York, NY
Norton Family Foundation, Santa Monica, CA
Ohio State University, Columbus, OH
Progressive Corporation, Mayfield, OH
San Diego Museum of Art, San Diego, CA
Santa Barbara Museum of Art, Santa Barbara, CA
The Stuart Collection, University of California, San Diego, La Jolla, CA
Hammer Museum, University of California, Los Angeles, CA
Walker Art Center, Minneapolis, MN
The Walt Disney Company, Los Angeles, CA

AWARDS

1995 Residency, The Rockefeller Foundation Study Center, Bellagio, Italy

1987 Fellowship Grant, National Endowment for the Arts

1986 Fourth Councilmanic District Civic Service Award, Los Angeles, CA

1983 Key to the City, Grand Rapids, MI

1976 Fellowship Grant, National Endowment for the Arts

1974 New Talent Award, Los Angeles County Museum of Art, Los Angeles, CA

TEACHING EXPERIENCE

1996 California Institute for the Arts, Valencia, CA
1993 Southern Methodist University, Dallas, TX, Meadows Distinguished Visiting Professor
1990 Skowhegan School of Painting and Sculpture, Skowhegan, ME
1985-88 University of California, Los Angeles, CA
1983 Kendall School of Design, artist-in-residence
1979-82 University of California, Los Angeles, CA
1977-78 University of California, San Diego, CA
1976 University of California, Irvine, CA
1975 California Institute of the Arts, Valencia, CA

The artist would like to acknowledge the help and support of the following people:

Dorsey Waxter and all the staff of Lawrence Rubin · Greenberg Van Doren · Fine Art, New York; Margo Leavin, Wendy Brandow, and all the staff of Margo Leavin Gallery, Los Angeles; Scott Grieger; Mary Ann Frericks; Michael Hogarth and all the craftsmen at Jerry Solomon Pictures Frames, Los Angeles; Norm Laich of L.A. Design Signs; Jeff Wasserman of Wasserman Silkscreen, Santa Monica; Doug Parker and Fran Solomon of Douglas M. Parker Studio, Los Angeles; Jimmy Isenson and the staff at L.A. Packing and Crating

Alexis Smith *An Embarrassment of Riches*

Edited by Augusto Arbizo and Belinda Marcus
Production by Paola Gribaudo
Photography by Douglas M. Parker Studio, Los Angeles, CA

Lawrence Rubin · Greenberg Van Doren · Fine Art
730 Fifth Avenue, at 57th Street
New York NY 10019
212-445-0444 TELEPHONE
212-445-0442 FAX
lrgvd@lrgvd.com EMAIL

© 2001 Alexis Smith, all artworks

© 2001 Lawrence Rubin · Greenberg Van Doren · Fine Art
New York, NY. All rights reserved. No part of the contents of this catalogue may be reproduced without the written permission of the publisher.

ISBN 0-9677573-7-1

Printed and bound in Italy by Pozzo Gros Monti
Color separations: Fotolito Garbero